The Weather of Love

Yolynda Bradshaw

Presentation by *BookLeaf Publishing*

Web: www.bookleafpub.com

E-mail: info@bookleafpub.com

ISBN: 9789357614078

First edition 2022

I Saw you

I saw you from a distance
Your tallness
Your boldness
Your integrity
I read your lips
The movement so engaging like looking at
honey in a honeycomb
Words flowing out spiritual healing of sensitivity
to kindness
I can never forget your flow of water that never
runs dry
Day after day
Seeing you at a distance
I took that leap of faith
Walking with confidence of a lifetime
Slow motion it was
Flowing out of your arms a drop of paper
The opportunity to take it
To put it back in your manly arms
Locking eye to eye
I smile
A touch of skin sizzled my body like electric
current
Slow motion to present
While thanking me he took my hand
Saying

I saw you from a distance
You are virtuous
Your independence
Your worth
I read your lips
The movement mesmerizing like looking at
strawberries dip in chocolate
Words flowing out knowledge of compassion of
sensitivity to love
I can never forget your flow of water that never
runs dry
Day after day
Seeing you at a distance
I took that leap of faith
Walking with boldness of a century
Slow motion it was
Decided to let go of the paper
You grabbed it
To put it back in my manly arms
Locking eye to eye
I smile
A touch of skin sizzled my body like dynamite
I had to thank you for being my wife

My Happiness

I searched it
I found it
It was in the skies
The heavens showed me
The sun shined on me
The wind directed me
The rain flooded from my eyes
The air whisked it all away
The world spoke to me
This part of my life is happiness
For the birds sang to me
The trees rejoice in triumphant
Singing to me a new song
Walked the clouds of glory
This part of my life is happiness
Within it all a partner was found
My sunset
My rainbow
My strawberries
My happiness

The Pain

The pain
Sometimes it controls me
Water drops fall from my eyes
Doesn't have a care where it goes
Boldly taking a risk to free itself
No matter where it lands
A helping hand wipes it away
Diminishing the sadness
Just let my own tears fall
Let me follow my own tears to boldness
Set myself free from the pain
Take control of me
Be the happiness I can be
The pain
It's part of me
But I must let the water drops fall
Create my own sea
So that my soul can be made free
This is my story
My tears became the sea
And I am fierce to control it

Bittersweet

Something isn't right
Disconnected puzzle pieces
You lost me
You led me through the dark forest
Touched but I was alone
Willing but I was lost
I fell for you
You led me to destruction
It was bittersweet for you
A laugh in your heart
Anger in mines
Fresh fruit for you
Used seed for me
A dish serve cold
Disconnected puzzle pieces
Straight forward was best
A combat
I led you through the dark forest
Touched and you're excitedly clueless
Willing and you're able to climb
Given you the fruit of hunger
Life took its course
You saw your own destruction
Connected puzzle pieces
That's my bittersweet

I Rise up

Early morning
The sun called me
To rise up
His glory shine on me
I smile
The sun blessed me
Stepping outside
The breeze hugged me
The birds came to sing to me
I'm no Cinderella
Open your eyes
Open your mind
It already has happened to you

Beautiful Skies

I saw the eagles
They soar without a care in the world
Free to roam the beautiful skies
Flying by so swiftly between the clouds
Plunging down like a warrior without a shield
Not afraid to be caught in a trap
Grabbing hold to its prey with vengeance
Swallowing with pride of satisfaction
Happiness lingers beneath its wings
Ready to take flight on a new adventure
He that dwelleth in the skies
Is in refuge of His amazing love

Sing to You

I sing to you like poetry
Uplifting your soul to make it your own
My words heal you
Your smile embraces me
My knowledge electrifies you
Leading towards your loving arms of like
You won't let me down
For if you do
Your emotions will spill out like rain
Bringing forth the sunshine to make it my day
Do you hear the music
Poetry soul that makes us one
I sing to you like poetry
Together we are one in glory

My Own Storm

I was a thunderstorm
Ready to flash like lightening
Never a care to whom it touch
Strike to the ground I'm comforted
Cloudy skies turned my mouth to frown
Wind blows in every direction
For my mind is tormented
Save me from my own storm
Save me from me
Can my harm be undone
The skies began to clear
The mountain heard it's name
For I was cast away like another day
I should have taken control
For I let the day go by
And lose my own soul

Our Emotions

Our emotions filter our vibes
My eyes meet yours like shining stars in the sky
No need to make a wish
For the flowers grows from the very ground and
sprung for the world to see
That's us
Tears cried like orange juices
You kissed them away
We dance and twirl like rose petals falling softly
Angry like chopping watermelons
But victoriously delicious fruit bowl
We will forever love each other
For everything about you is poetry

Experiencing Quietness

I know not what the deaf is feeling
Being ignored by societies existence
Experiencing quietness
Noise unheard of
Living in happiness with hand expressions
Laughter of hope within the soul
Cravings of noise never to be known
The deaf may look alone
They aren't like thunderstorms
They are like the stars that twinkle at night
A gift from the Heavens
A life they can save
Feeling of alertness
Drive to succeed
Birds may lose one leg
But they still have its wings
So are the deaf
Never was different
Just unique in their beautiful rainbow
They will catch you before you fall
Believe it
They are here just like you until..

I am a Flower

I am a flower,
Soft yet strong,
Aromatic scent that lingers to your
remembrance,
Being twigged in every direction to your
satisfaction,
Wishing you would look at me with elegance
and not a breakable soul,
Tears of rain falling down on my sensitive
petals,
Bringing me back to revival
The sun heats me in beauty
Uplifting my everlasting wings of freedom,
I know I'm not one to brag,
My softness is all I have,
So take me as I am with delicacy,
Pour me in water with love,
Yes I'm delicate, but powerfully growing

I am a Woman

I'm strong like poetry
I'm tender hearted like the dolphins
I'm brave like a lioness
I'm loved by the singing birds
To stand tall like the trees
Soft to the touch like rose petals
I'm the light that shines for all
I am woman
Fierce beyond measure
Wrap your arms around me like the garden
Give back sunshine with a smile
I am woman
Sexy and divine
Created to be virtuous
To love forever

You are Amazing

Silent sky, gleaming moon
One way to describe you
Sunny lips, beautiful mind
Ohhh your so divine
Lost in thought
Mesmerize like the night skies
Urgency to join you
In knowledge and wisdom
You hold an authority
Strong and mighty
Praying to God to hold you in His love
Playing harp like a flowing flying dove
You're amazing in my eyes
Take me to intellectual words
Wrapped in my soul, pure in heart
Silent sky, gleaming moon
You are my one and only tune.

Be Free

I have been squeezed lately
By you that won't let me go
It's been rough around the edges
Mine wasted on you
Holding me back to the past
Trapped me naked of betrayals
Hiding, but I know I can be set free
My mine playing tricks on me
My eyes open
Found myself outside
Freely naked in all its glory
Being in a hard and rigid place
The tree protected me from me
Too hardheaded to admit
I was already free
It's only me that wouldn't let go
I love it here
Uncomfortable has it may be
I will still love me anyway
It wasn't always you
It was me

Field of Dandelions

I lay outside in a field of dandelions.
Looking up towards the sky I told Him
I'm broken, but I'm beautiful
Feeling hollow on the inside
Broken like petals of flower
Stooped down low
Wishing for someone to sing me lullabies
Dancing while the sunrise
This would be a lovely surprise
I smile
This is my time to shine
I might as well give this a try
I must rise
If a broken heart can mend
Then I'm no longer broken
For the beautiful sea continues without end
I danced amongst the dandelions
I sang like an instrument until…
I'm beautiful and free

A Story

In every human mind
There is a story
A sad one
A happy one
A lonely one
A terrible one
A secret is hard to keep
Tell it like a story
It sets you free
You may feel damage
You may feel neglect
The words give meaning
Hope that never fails
So…..
Tell your secret
Explore your mind
Say it all
Save a soul
Be free

Come Fly with Me

Come fly away with me
I want to ride to the moon
Hang out with the stars
Settle in the quiet
Nothing to block me
No one to chastise me
Only me and nature
No need to pretend
Speaking to Him in the clouds
All His glory shining through
No need to wish upon a star
For they know my heart desires
Sleep amongst the good
Awake in the arms of the sunset
No need to write my words
I can sing to Him in poetry
Earth is far from my mind
Stay here
To be peaceful
Taking it all in
One night at a time
To leave it all
No not ever
Come fly away with me
You won't regret to see His sight
Meditate until the rise of the sunlight

Play Me Jazz

Play me jazz
Play me jazz
Light the candles
Dim the lights
Love to hear jazz every other night
Memories of yesterday
Floating through my brain
Only smiles I merely can't contain
Play me jazz
Play me jazz
Bring back my smile
To set the night
Light the candles
Dim the lights
This is our mood
Puts us in a groove
One step two step
We're in the right tune
Together forever
My friend til the end

Under the Oak Tree

I come to you on this day
To tell you how much I care
No matter where you are
No matter where you've been
Tell me your story
We'll sit under the oak tree
Listen to the birds sing
Inhale the untreated world
Exhale the torments of the earth
For we wish the rain to fall
Draining the toxic down to sea
Time after time
We'll catch each other's fall
Be each other's hero and stand tall
Seek truth
Confront lies
Together we won't be hypnotized
Time after time
We'll sit under the oak tree
Be ourselves the way we want to be
For Heaven is watching
Both you and me
Live free
But positively

Marry Me

Marry me
Say yes
I'm the beautiful ocean
Captivated by the clouds of glory
Walking towards intelligence
A mind growing sunflower
Guiding through motivation
Uplifting each other with inspiration
Have mercy upon each other
Argumentative comments
Meditation to calm our veins
Marry me
Say yes
My eyes seeks out your knowledge
My body melts to your integrity
Swimming like school fishes together in the sea
How happy we will be
Don't follow the scared.
Don't follow the proud.
Don't follow the lonely.
Follow the harp that spring forth melodies
My heart
Your heart
Will you marry me
Say yes

My Dream of Jazz

You came to me in a dream
Jazz playing from a distance
The music saw me
It twirl itself around me
Whispered in my ears saying
Gorgeously delicious
The music made me high
It took me to the mountain top
Slowly back to valleys low
I smelt like strawberries
It's juices lingered
Awaiting the music to give its rhythm
The moment was captured like a picture
I shivered like the cold
The music played on
And I was it's tune
It wanted more
Jazz enlightened my mind
Playing the instrument of knowledge
Consuming all my wisdom from my mind
It fell in love
Wouldn't let go
For we were in sync in lyrics
The music suddenly went out of tune
I awoke from out of the blue

Soft jazz playing
I smiled
The jazz was worth playing for